IF YOU WERE A

HORSE

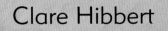
Clare Hibbert

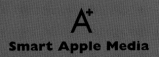
Smart Apple Media

Published in the United States by Smart Apple Media
PO Box 3263, Mankato, Minnesota 56002

Editor: Joe Harris
Picture researcher: Clare Hibbert
Designer: Emma Randall

Picture credits:
All images courtesy of Shutterstock.

Library of Congress Cataloging-in-Publication Data

Hibbert, Clare, 1970-
 If you were a horse / Clare Hibbert.
    p. cm. -- (If you were a--)
 Audience: Grade 4 to 6.
 Summary: "Describes features, life, and habits of horses, and contrasts them with human
life"-- Provided by publisher.
 Includes bibliographical references and index.
 ISBN 978-1-59920-964-7 (library binding)
1. Horses--Juvenile literature. 2. Horses--Behavior--Juvenile literature. I. Title. II. Title:
Horse.
 QL737.U6H53 2014
 636.1--dc23
                            2013002972

Printed in China

Supplier 03, Date 0513, Print Run 2370
SL002677US

Contents

Horse Senses

If you were a horse, you might stand taller or smaller than a person. Whatever kind of horse you were, you'd be designed for galloping fast and keeping up with the herd. You would rely on your sharp senses to detect danger and find out about your surroundings.

Looking Around

Horses' eyes are set far up on the sides of the skull, so they have good all-around vision apart from a few small blind spots. Horses can pick out details from 30 feet (9 m) away, while humans only see detail from 20 feet (6 m) away.

Smell

Horses have large nostrils for taking in great lungfuls of air. Scent particles in the air give horses lots of useful information. Smell is especially important for figuring out whether food is good or bad to eat.

Horse Questions

Q: Why does my horse curl its lip?
A: This strange snarling is called flehmening. Horses do it to expose a special sense organ under the upper lip, the Jacobsen's organ, to scent particles from the air.

Sensitive Hairs

Horses have a velvety, sensitive muzzle that is covered in whiskery hairs. These hairs, and the whiskers around the eyes, help horses to sense nearby objects and investigate through touch.

Horse Eyes

If you were a horse, your eyes would be your early warning system. Each of your eyes could take in about a semicircle of your surroundings. Your eyes would allow you to spot danger approaching, even when your head was lowered for grazing.

How Horses See

Horses see the world in shades of yellow and blue. The retina (the part of their eyes that senses light) contains only two types of cones, which detect color. Humans have three types of cones and see in three colors—red, yellow, and blue.

"Night Sight"

Horses have much better vision in dim light than humans, thanks to a mirrored layer at the back of the eye. However, it takes horses' eyes longer to adjust when moving between bright light and darkness—as long as 15 minutes!

Revealing Eyes

Eyes are not only for seeing—they also express horses' moods. If you can see the whites of a horse's eyes, it is feeling afraid or aggressive. A horse with large, open eyes is probably calm and relaxed.

Horse Questions

Q: Where are horses' blind spots?
A: Horses have 350-degree vision. Their blind spots are the area directly behind their body that is the width of the head and the areas just above the eyes and below the nose.

Ears and Hearing

If you were a horse, you'd have long, mobile (movable) ears. They would be for more than simply hearing—they would also act as signposts. The position of your ears would communicate your mood to the other animals around you.

Horse Hearing

In the wild, horses are hunted. Like most prey animals, they have excellent hearing. They can pick up higher-pitched sounds than humans can, and they are more finely tuned in to noises that could signal danger, such as snapping twigs.

More Clues

Ears even give away what horses are thinking about! Alert horses tend to point their ears toward whatever their attention is focused on. So, when a gate opens, the horses in a field will all point their ears in that direction.

Horse Questions

Q: What does it mean if one of my horse's ears is pointing forward and the other back?
A: Each of a horse's ears can move independently. When a horse is feeling uncertain, its ears will point different ways.

Revealing Ears

If a horse's ears are flattened straight back, the animal is angry. If the ears are pointing backward, the horse is afraid. Upright but relaxed ears show that the horse is feeling content and cooperative.

Body Language

If you were a horse, your body's posture and movements would reveal a lot about your mood. They would show whether you were feeling relaxed, playful, or impatient. You would also know how to "read" the body language of the horses in your herd, field, or stable.

All in the Pose

How an animal holds its body is called posture. Horses that feel safe and content have a relaxed posture and hold their bodies low and stretched out. Horses that feel nervous have a tense, taut posture.

Go Away!

When horses want to be left alone, they usually just turn their back on other horses or people. Horses are not often aggressive, but raising the hind legs is a clear threat. That's the moment to steer clear of them—or risk being kicked.

A Show of Strength

Stallions may sometimes rear up on their hind legs and stick out their front legs. This is their way of showing how big and powerful they are. It might be a real threat—or it might be a young horse playing at being big and strong.

Horse Questions

Q: Why do horses shake their heads?
A: When horses do this while baring their teeth, they are showing aggression. More usually, though, head shaking is a sign of irritation—especially if it is accompanied by some impatient foot stamping.

Horse Talk

If you were a horse, most of your communication would be silent and revealed through your posture and actions. However, you would also "talk" to other horses and people using noises such as neighs, whinnies, snorts, and whickers.

Horsey Hello

Horses enjoy company. If their owner appears or a new horse joins them in the field, they will usually approach with a friendly neigh. The neigh is a greeting—it means "Hello!" and "Welcome!"

Horse Questions

Q: Do mothers talk to their foals?
A: Dams (mother horses) worry when they are separated from their foals and use a noise called a "whicker" or "nicker" to call them back. They also whinny or neigh "hello" to their foals.

Snorting

Horses snort when they are excited or fearful. In the wild, the snort is a signal to other members of the herd. It means: "Watch out! There's danger around! Get ready to run!"

Look at Me!

The whinny is an attention-seeking noise. Stallions whinny to show that they are dominant (powerful) or if they can smell a nearby mare. Whinnying can be a sign of frustration or boredom, too.

Friendship

If you were a horse, companionship would be important to you. You'd form lifelong friendships with other horses that you spent time with. Without the company of other horses, you might become withdrawn and lose the ability to communicate properly.

Best Friends

Horses that are friends often stand close together. Sometimes they are head-to-head, nuzzling muzzles. Sometimes they are head-to-tail, rubbing manes and using their tails to swat flies out of each other's faces!

Horse Questions

Q: Can horses grieve?

A: Horses form strong attachments. If a horse's companion dies or moves away, the horse will often show signs of grief. He or she may be bad-tempered or listless for a while. This mood change may even be long-lasting.

Playtime

Horses are playful animals. Even as adults, they enjoy games with their friends. Mares especially like chasing and racing each other. Play reinforces the bonds of friendship and is a good way to enjoy some exercise, too.

Play-Fighting

Male horses—stallions and geldings—are often rivals but sometimes friends. Males play-fight—rearing up, circling, and even biting. Play-fights look dangerous, but there are strict rules, and the horses don't really hurt each other.

Feeding

If you were a horse, you'd be a grazing animal and your main food would be grass or hay. You would have to eat almost all day long because your small stomach would not hold much food. Your food would contain some water, but you'd need fresh drinking water, too.

Constant Eating

Horses need access to grass or hay most of the time. In the wild, they spend at least 15 hours grazing each day. Their guts are designed to digest a constant supply of roughage rather than a few large meals.

Daily Diet

Grass and hay contain roughage, or fiber. Depending on how much grazing horses are able to do, they may need hay as well. Most horses also have a daily portion of oats. Some are given a supplement containing extra fiber.

Horse Questions

Q: What treats do horses like?
A: Crunchy fruit and vegetables, such as apples or carrots, sugar cubes, and whole wheat bread all make ideal treats for horses. It's best to offer a treat on the flat palm of your hand.

Life in the Desert

Mustangs are wild horses that live in American grasslands and deserts. Their ancestors were domesticated horses that escaped. Mustangs have adapted to tough living conditions. They can go without food for a few days—and sometimes chew cacti for moisture!

Grooming

If you were a horse, you would rely on your owner to keep you clean—and your horse friends. In return, you would groom other horses. You'd nibble at the places they could not reach themselves and pick out parasites or clumps of mud.

Sign of Friendship

Mutual grooming is when two animals groom each other. It shows that they trust each other and helps to strengthen their friendship. Grooming horses use their teeth to pick out knots and dirt, and to scratch at itchy bits of skin.

Horse Questions

Q: Where do horses like to be scratched?
A: Horses love to be scratched in hard-to-reach places, such as the withers or under the mane. They show their enjoyment by half-closing their eyes and leaning into the scratch!

Tools of the Trade

Grooming cleans the coat and also massages horses' muscles. Owners use a rubber "curry comb" to remove any dried mud, then a wire "dandy brush" to loosen stray hairs, and finally, a softer body brush to make the coat glossy.

Dustbath

Horses do have one way of caring for their own coat—rolling in dust! The dirt helps to get rid of loose hairs and parasite eggs. Horses enjoy rolling, and it also gives them a shared "herd smell", because they use the same rolling spot.

Running Free

If you were a horse, you'd be excellent at running. You'd enjoy galloping along just for the fun of it, with the wind in your mane. You'd also have an inbuilt impulse to run away from the first sign of danger, just like your wild cousins and ancestors.

The Flight Impulse

The horse's distant ancestors were prey animals living on the grasslands of Africa. Horses had to be cautious in order to survive. To this day, untrained horses are easily startled and take flight if they sense danger.

Stampede

When horses "spook" (get startled), they shy away or jump to the side and snort. If the source of their fear continues, they take flight. When a whole herd of horses spook at the same time, there's a stampede.

Horse Questions

Q: Do all horses spook?
A: Horses can be brought up so they don't spook at everyday noises. That means they stay calm rather than take flight when they hear sounds such as dogs barking or cars honking.

Running at Top Speed

Horses have four different paces. From slowest to fastest they are the walk, trot, canter, and gallop. Each has its own pattern of hoof beats. Galloping is the most exciting pace—racehorses can reach 44 miles per hour (72 km/h).

Resting

If you were a horse, you would need to take time out. Grazing, sunbathing, and playing would be your ways of unwinding, and you would need to nap or sleep, too. Even when you were really relaxed, you would still be quick to run if you heard a sudden noise.

Standing at Rest

Horses take most of their weight on their front legs. Sometimes they give each of their back legs a rest in turn, so the muscles can really relax. They stand so the toe of the resting leg just touches the ground.

Just Napping

Horses can doze standing up. First, they "lock" their hind leg joints so they won't fall over. Dozing horses half-close their eyes, slacken their mouth, and let their head and neck droop. Their heartbeat slows a little, too.

Horse Questions

Q: Do horses dream?
A: Horses only dream during deep sleep—a state that lasts just 15 minutes or so. When horses dream, their legs jerk, their eyes move, and they may moan, snort, or neigh.

Sleeping

Horses lie down to sleep. For light sleep, they keep all four legs pulled up beneath their body, so they can spring to their feet in an instant. In deep sleep, horses stretch straight out on their side. They only do this if there's another horse acting as lookout.

Mother and Foal

If you were a horse, you'd have started life as a foal. You would have developed inside your mother for almost a year until you were ready to be born. Like all mammal babies, you would have fed on your mother's milk.

Up on their Feet

Human babies are born helpless, but foals can stand and walk within an hour of their birth—though they are a little wobbly. In just 24 hours, they can trot or gallop. Being able to move with the herd is essential for survival in the wild.

Foal Food

Foals start to suckle in their first couple of hours. The dam's first milk, colostrum, is especially rich and also helps the foal to fight disease. Foals can eat grass at a few weeks old, but they continue to drink milk for up to a year.

Horse Questions

Do foals have toys?
A: Young horses love to play with other foals. If there are no other youngsters, they will find toys to play with instead. Anything they can kick or paw or chew counts as a toy!

New Life

Mares usually give birth to a single foal. Sometimes, very rarely, they have twins. In the wild, pregnancy is timed so that foals are born in the spring, when there is plenty of grass for both mothers and babies to eat.

Working Horses

If you were a horse, you'd be used to living with people—and making yourself useful to them. Whatever your lifestyle and workload, you'd belong to a breed built for the job. You'd really enjoy being praised by your human companions or coworkers.

Horses for Riding

Riding schools keep horses that adults and children can learn to ride. Some offer lessons for people with special needs. Whether they are able-bodied or disabled, riders experience a sense of freedom when they're on horseback.

Horses for Sports

Horse racing, where horses try to outrun each other on flat courses or steeplechases, is not only popular—it's also big business. The horses themselves can cost millions of dollars, and in some countries, gambling on the race results is allowed.

Showing Off

Dressage is a sport where horses and their riders show off their jumps and other skills in an arena. The famous gray Lipizzaner stallions entertain people all over the world. Their shows have been described as "horse ballet"!

Horse Questions

Q: How do horses help people do their jobs?
A: Before the days of engines, horses did all kinds of jobs, from pulling carts to dragging farm machinery. Even today, there are still cowboys, police officers, and soldiers who ride as part of their job.

Horse and Rider

If you were a horse that people rode, you'd understand certain commands. You'd also be used to wearing the equipment (tack) that kept your rider safe and made you easier to control. You'd know how to behave well, and in return, your owner would look after you.

Top Tack

As youngsters, horses become accustomed to wearing a bridle or halter, bit, and reins. These pieces of equipment allow the horse to be led, halted, or turned. Horses also get used to the saddle and stirrups that hold the rider on their back.

Horse Questions

Q: Why does my horse sigh?
A: When a horse sighs, it's not being touchy. Gentle blowing through the nose is really a sign of contentment. Horses sometimes sigh when you praise them.

Commands

Horses learn to obey a number of spoken commands. They recognize some of the words themselves—for example, "Walk on!" or "Whoa!" However, they also respond to the tone in which the words are said.

Teamwork

In return for their hard work and loyalty, horses are rewarded with praise, fun, and companionship. They can also rely on their owners for life's necessities—food and shelter—and for care when they get sick.

Glossary

ancestor A member of the family that lived long ago.

bit The part of the bridle that goes inside the horse's mouth.

blind spot The place where an animal cannot see, due to the position of its eyes.

bridle A piece of horse headgear, made up of leather straps.

colostrum The rich, first milk that a mammal mother produces after the birth of her offspring.

cooperative Willing to do what someone wants.

curry comb A square, rectangular, or oval comb with rubber or plastic teeth, used for grooming horses.

dam A mother horse.

dandy brush A brush with harsh, wiry bristles, used for grooming horses. The brush handle is usually oval and made of wood.

digest To break down food.

domesticated Describes an animal that is used to living alongside people, rather than in the wild.

flehmening Opening the mouth and curling the upper lip to expose the Jacobsen's organ.

gelding A male horse that has had an operation so that it cannot produce offspring.

halter A simple piece of horse headgear, usually made of rope.

Jacobsen's organ A sense organ that detects chemicals and scents.

listless Lifeless; not wanting to do anything.

mare An adult female horse.

muzzle The protruding part of an animal's face that includes the nose and mouth.

parasite An animal that lives on another animal and relies on it for food.

prey An animal that is hunted by other animals for food. In the wild, horses are prey for meat-eating animals such as lions or wolves.

rival A competitor. Male horses are often rivals, competing for the attention of females.

roughage Fiber from grasses and other long-stemmed plants.

stallion An adult male horse that is able to produce offspring.

stampede When a large number of animals all run in the same direction at the same time.

steeplechase A horse race over an obstacle course or open country.

supplement Something that supplies something extra. Food supplements provide extra nourishment, for example. Sugar beet supplements are given to horses to give them extra fiber.

taut Stretched or tightened. The opposite of loose.

withers The top of a horse's shoulder blade.

Further Reading

Complete Horse Care Manual by Colin Vogel (Dorling Kindersley, 2011)

How to Speak "Horse": A Horse-Crazy Kid's Guide to Reading Body Language, Understanding Behavior, and "Talking Back" with Simple Groundwork Lessons by Andrea Eschbach and Markus Eschbach (Trafalgar Square Books, 2012)

Illustrated Horse and Pony Encyclopedia by Sandy Ransford (Kingfisher, 2010)

The United States Pony Club Manual of Horsemanship: Basics for Beginners/D Level by Susan E. Harris (Howell Book House, 2012)

Web Sites

animals.nationalgeographic.com/animals/mammals/przewalskis-horse/
Information on Przewalski's horse from National Geographic.

http://animal.discovery.com/guides/horses/horses.html
An Animal Planet channel guide to horse breeds, training, and care.

http://equinewelfarealliance.org/Children_s_Page.html
Find out all about horse welfare from the Equine Welfare Alliance web site, packed with facts, pictures, and videos.

http://www.aspca.org/pet-care/horse-care/
A guide to looking after your horse or pony from the animal care charity, the ASPCA.

http://www.humanesociety.org/animals/horses/
Learn all about protecting wild and domestic horses across the United States.

Index